W9-DFM-359

MAINE COON

Mimy Sluiter

MAINE COON

REBO
PUBLISHERS

© 2003 Zuid Boekprodukties
© 2006 Rebo Publishers

Text: Mimy Sluiter
Photographs: Marian Draat, Furry Tails.nl/Esther Verhoef, Marga Harms,
Astrid and Leo Straver and Francien Verspui
Cover design: Minkowsky Graphic Design, Enkhuizen, The Netherlands
Layout: AdAm Studio, Prague, The Czech Republic
Typesetting and pre-press services: Artedit s.r.o., Prague The Czech Republic

ISBN 13: 978-90-366-1549-5
ISBN 10: 90-366-1549-6

All rights reserved. No part of this publication may be reproduced, stored in
or introduced into a retrieval system, or transmitted in any form or by any
means (electronic, mechanical, photocopying,recording or otherwise), without the prior permission of both the copyright owners and the publisher of
this book.

CONTENTS

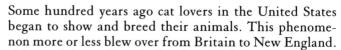

1 THE HISTORY OF THE MAINE COON

Earliest Cats

Some hundred years ago cat lovers in the United States began to show and breed their animals. This phenomenon more or less blew over from Britain to New England. Many of the well-to-do families on the East Coast had English ancestors and the luxury ships available to them made it possible to stay in contact with their English family and friends. Many young English ladies attended American balls, where they found husbands. Along with the dowry, thoroughbred cats were often shipped directly to the States. Most of them were longhaired cats, of the breed that today is known as the Persian. But on the East Coast of the United States they also had their own beautiful longhaired domestic cats. At the time, their beauty certainly matched that of the English Persians, whose noses were not nearly as short as they are today. These local longhairs were called Maine Cats or Maine Coons.

Blue Maine Coon kitten in about 1900

The Origin of the Maine Coon Cat

The origin of the Maine Coon cat is not very well documented. All we know from ships' inventories is that for centuries, since the very earliest European colonizations, cats were taken from Europe to the United States. Approximately ten percent of English cats are longhaired, but the percentage is much higher in the region where the Maine Coon originated. This higher percentage might be

A nineteenth century Maine Coon

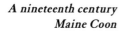

explained by the fact that longhaired cats exported from England would have been more immune to the fairly harsh wintry climate in Vermont and Maine than their shorthaired counterparts. In addition, most people considered longhaired cats more chic than shorthaired cats. It is, therefore, quite possible that relatively more longhaired cats were imported, or that they received better care than shorthaired ones.

Breed Name

There are two explanations for the name Maine Coon. Its often ringed tail used to lead people to believe that it was a cross between a cat and a raccoon. Of course, we now know that this is genetically impossible. Another story that explains the breed name is that of an English cat-loving ship captain, called Coon. He used to sail to New England, with longhaired cats on board. Whenever he went ashore, his cats used to go with him, and some of them never returned to the ship. When longhaired kittens started appearing in litters born in the American state of

Maine, the queen's owners called them "Coon cats," descendents of Captain Coon's cats.

The Beginning

The first cat shows were held in the United States around the turn of the twentieth century. Initially, a distinction was made between two types of longhaired cats; the "Maine Cats" on the one hand and the animals imported from Britain–the Persians–on the other. The distinction was not evident at the shows; both the English Persians and the Maine Cats were grouped together as "long haired." Their origin was listed in the catalogues, however, and registered in the pedigree. While both the English and the American cats could be registered, there was one subtle difference: American cats could only be registered if a sworn statement could be submitted certifying that both parents were also longhaired. Registering the origin of the cats was customary until about 1915. The Maine Coons were then merged with the English longhaired variety to form a single longhaired Persian breed. Maine Coons were no longer bred as an independent breed.

In the early days of American cat shows, there was no distinction between Persians and Maine Coons

*Brown tabby Maine
Coon in about 1900*

Official Recognition

It was to be another fifty years or so before there was a renewed interest in the authentic American Maine Coon. Not all Maine Coons had ended up in the breeding circuit. Consequenty many were not "absorded" into the Persian breed. Living as pets or farm cats on the East Coast, some of them had managed to stay true to the breed, even though their owners often kept no pedigree or had failed to keep it up to date. In 1950 two ladies in Maine set up the Central Maine Cat Club. They began to promote the Maine Coon as an authentic American breed. It was to be another ten years before the first authentic Maine Coons were to make their entrance at American shows in the 1960s. Enthusiasts started keeping record of pedigrees again, registering their animals with the feline thoroughbred organizations. The American cat lovers proudly presented the breed as their own "native breed" and the cat was officially proclaimed the "state animal" of Maine. In 1976 the breed was recognized by the American organization, the Cat Fanciers Association (CFA). Before then though, several smaller associations had already recognized the breed so that, logically, many Maine Coon lovers and breeders had registered with them. These smaller associations later became one large thoroughbred cat federation: TICA (The International Cat Association). So it is hardly surprising that among its members the TICA has many Maine Coon lovers and breeders, who have remained faithful to the association to this day.

Europe

The first Maine Coons arrived in Europe in the early 1980s. They first appeared at cat shows in Germany, shortly followed by the Netherlands and other European countries. The recognition by the largest association in Europe, the Federation International Féline (FIFé), came soon after that, during the AGM in Wiesbaden in late 1982. The recognition became officially effective on January 1, 1983. There was no stopping the breed's success in Europe now. In next to no time, the Maine Coon became extremely popular in practically every country in Europe. A consistent supply of cats imported from the

*A cat show
in the late
nineteenth
century*

United States created a large stock of Maine Coons, in all possible colors. In some countries, the Maine Coon has even surpassed the Persian in terms of popularity.

*White Maine
Coon kitten*

2 EXTERNAL FEATURES

Breed Standard

The breed standard the cat associations maintain for the Maine Coon is practically identical the world over. Most of these standards are based on the American CFA breed standard, given below. The Maine Coon breed standard reflects a natural breed. This means that no crossbreeding with any other breed is accepted. It also means that any colors and/or patterns that are not inherent to the breed (such as colors and patterns of oriental origin) are unacceptable.

Profile of a silver tabby queen

General

The Maine Coon was originally a sturdy farm cat, tough enough to cope with a rough climate. One of the cat's characteristic features is its smooth, shaggy coat. It is a well-proportioned and well-balanced animal; not a thing about it is exaggerated. The Maine Coon has a friendly nature and finds it easy to adapt to many different circumstances and surroundings.

Head

Another characteristic feature is the head, which is of medium width and has a square muzzle. Older toms can develop jowls, making the head look much broader. High jaws, and a strong chin in line with the nose and top lip are very important. The nose is of medium length, and

Maine Coon tom,
black blotched

has a gentle concave curve when viewed from the front. The large ears are wide at the base with a good amount of hair on the inside. They taper to a fairly pointed tip, and are set approximately an ear's width apart at the base, with no flare. The eyes are large, expressive, and widely set. The setting is slightly oblique, the outside corner should point towards the ear. The neck is of average length.

Body

The Maine Coon is medium to large in size with a muscular body and a broad chest. Queens are generally smaller than toms. The body is long with all parts in harmonious proportion, creating a well-balanced, rectangular appearance: not a single part of the cat's anatomy is exaggerated enough to disturb the balance. Maine Coons

Maine Coon kittens, silver tabby and blue

develop slowly. The legs are strong, wide set and medium in length, matching the body. The front legs are straight; the back legs are straight when viewed from behind. The cat should have big, round, well-tufted paws, with five toes at the front and four at the back. The tail is long, wide at the base, and should taper to the tip. The tail fur is long and flowing.

Coat

The coat is thick and shaggy. It is shorter on the shoulders and longer on the belly and back. A ruff is preferable. The texture is silky and the coat lies close to the body. Too short a coat, or one that is the same length all over, is considered a fault.

Grounds for disqualification

A delicate bone structure, undershot mouth, crossed-eyes, a kink in the tail, or wrong number of toes can all lead to disqualification. Cats with evidence of cross-breeding resulting in the colors chocolate/lilac, points, or ticked tabby are all deemed unacceptable.

Coat Colors and the Standard

The standard for the general breed type might be more or less the same worldwide. There are, however differences when it comes to the acceptable colors. Throughout the world, Maine Coons are bred in a wide range of color combinations and patterns, but the classification into color groups at shows, and the names given to these groups, can vary. Some shades are debatable and certainly not accepted everywhere. These include like chocolate, cinnamon, ticked tabby, and partial albino factors such as Siamese and Burmese coloring, that are only occasionally seen. Most breeders feel that these are not qualities of this authentic breed of farm cat.

> ## *Related breeds*
>
> *There are plenty of other longhaired "breeds of farm cat" besides the Maine Coon. The original types of those breeds are still to be found as sturdy farm cats or pets in their native country or region. For example, the Norwegian Forest Cat, from Norway, differs from the Maine Coon in its triangular-shaped head and lighter build (the back legs are longer than the front legs). From Russia, we have the Siberian Cat, with a fairly round head and a more compact body. And finally, in Turkey, you'll find the Turkish Angora, the slimmest of all longhaired farm cat breeds, with an elegant build and a fairly long, slender head.*

3 PRIOR CONSIDERATIONS

Why Choose a Maine Coon?

*Maine Coons
usually have
accommodating,
easygoing
characters*

Before you decide to buy a particular breed, it is important to know whether or not the breed will suit you in terms of character. One of the reasons the breed has become so popular is that the Maine Coon is not a cat for "advanced owners only." Maine Coons are renowned for their affectionate, quiet, and stable character and they get along well with children and dogs. They are faithful pets that grow attached to the entire family, although some tend to choose one particular person as their obvious favorite. They enjoy being a part of day today life at home, without ever being intrusive or too active. Harmony in the home is very important to them. They don't have a very loud voice, but they make up for it with a considerable vocabulary. This varies from quiet little "chirp" meows to a firm, dark "mow," enabling them to make themselves perfectly clear, in their contact with their own kind and with humans. A Maine Coon does well in a quiet, two-person household, but will usually settle equally well in a busy family with children and dogs. Every individual animal's character will, of course, vary from the general character attributed to the breed. Some will be quieter while others will be much livelier. Descriptions like "harmonious," "resilient," and "enjoys company," will, nevertheless, apply to most Maine Coons.

*Black silver
blotched kitten*

A Life Long

A Maine Coon is a loyal housemate. If you have one as a pet, you will know what it was that made you fall for that particular breed – the combination of the calm, stable character particular to the breed, plus its beautiful and robust appearance. However, keeping a pet also entails a lot of care and responsibility, something that should be taken into consideration beforehand. A well-bred Maine Coon is a healthy animal that can easily live to the age of fifteen. That means that for a significant part of your life, you will be responsible for its day-to-day care. Your Maine Coon is dependent on you and will rely on you to look after it. Besides the cost of good food and cat litter, (the tray must be cleaned regularly) there will also be the recurrent expense of things such as worming, repeat vaccinations and keeping both your cat and your home flea-free. In addition, there will be the veterinary fees, both expected and unexpected. Accidents can't always be avoided and no matter how well you care for your cat, it can still fall ill, and veterinary fees can add up. Your home furnishings will have to be feline friendly and you will need to be fairly tolerant. Not all cats sharpen their claws on a scratch post only, some like to try their luck on a chair leg or the stair carpet. Should your Maine Coon regurgitate a hairball, it shouldn't upset you too much if it chooses to do so on your brand new sofa. Kittens, and some adult cats too, sometimes urinate outside the cat tray, in a spot you'd rather they didn't. And, considering the Maine Coon's beautiful long coat, you should become accustomed to having to remove loose hairs from your furniture. The cat itself will, of course need regular brushing as well. If you plan a vacation, arrangements will have to be made to have a cat-sitter look after it or for it to go to a cattery. And finally, as with humans, age has its drawbacks and various ailments can occur as your cat gets older. These include gum problems, for example, but also more serious conditions like cancer or organ failure. You need to be there for your pet at all times.

A Kitten or an Adult Cat

Once people have decided to buy a pedigree cat, they usually prefer a kitten. This is because the owner wants to raise the cat himself and wants to watch the cat grow up. Most people also find kittens more endearing and the general opinion is that a young animal is better able to adapt to new surroundings. This reasoning, however well-founded, will not always apply. The cat's character, for instance is largely genetically determined. While most Maine Coons have a calm, well-balanced nature, some can be livelier and more high-spirited or quieter and shyer than average. With good, loving care from the breeder, and later from you, the cat's temperament and behavior can be modified and molded, but there is no changing the animal's nature.

Cream and white young tom

Bringing an Adult Cat into your Home

An adult Maine Coon can be just as good a buy if you do not have the time needed for the intensive care and upbringing of a kitten, for example, or if you are not so young yourself anymore and prefer not to have a cat for the whole of its (expected) life. Adult cats are often rehomed through the cat association or breed association. There are hundreds of reasons for rehoming adult cats, and contrary to what most people think, the problem is certainly not always the cat itself. Altered family circumstances or deteriorating health can sometimes mean that a person can no longer care for the cat adequately. Or perhaps the cat's character does not fit in with that of other cats in a large group. Sometimes a new home has to be found because the owner has died or the cat has become the innocent victim of divorce. Finally, some ex-studs can no longer return to an existing group once they have been neutered. Such a cat deserves a permanent new home. These situations arise frequently and the cat is not to blame. Behavioral problems such as lack of house-training or antisocial behavior are, of course, a different matter. But even then the surroundings and circumstances could be the cause. A cat that fails to flourish in a large group could blossom beautifully as a lone pet. The association arranging the rehoming is usually familiar with the rea-

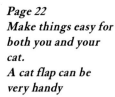

Page 22
Make things easy for both you and your cat.
A cat flap can be very handy

Instead of a kitten, you could choose an adult cat as your new housemate

A fenced garden, if you have the option, is great fun for your cat

Despite their somewhat cross expression, Maine Coons are actually very gentle and friendly

An adult cat will often take a little longer to settle

sons for the rehoming request. They will tell you exactly
what the reasons are, as neither they nor the cats they are
trying to rehome would benefit if the proposed mediation
ended in disappointment. If you go to see an adult cat with
the intent to rehome it, always make clear arrangements
as to what you should do if, for whatever reason, things
don't work out. However, an adult Maine Coon will usually settle in nicely in a new home and will soon become
quite attached to its new owners. The price of an adult cat
that needs rehoming will usually be much lower than the
price of a kitten. It is perfectly reasonable for the previous
owner to request compensation for the cost of neutering.

Tom or Queen?

As far as appearance is concerned, there is really only one
difference between a tom and a queen: Maine Coon toms
are usually a size bigger than the queens. But because the
Maine Coon is the largest breed of cat there is, the queens
are usually a fair size too. As far as their character is con-

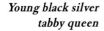

*Young black silver
tabby queen*

A Maine Coon tom is usually decidedly more impressive than a queen

cerned, there is a slight difference that really applies to all breeds of cat: toms are generally more easygoing, whereas queens tend to be a bit "catty." This behavioral difference has to do with the hormonal difference between a tom and a queen–and the difference will remain to a certain extent, even after a tom has been neutered. A good-natured Maine Coon tom will quite happily move out of her way if a queen makes it known that she wants to lie where he just happens to be lying. Reverse the situation, however, and the queen will make it perfectly clear that she is lying there and that the tom should find a bed elsewhere. Having said that though, Maine Coons of either sex are easy, sociable animals and extremely tolerant of people, other cats, and pets in general. The choice of a tom or queen is, therefore, not terribly important, either will make perfectly good pets. It is, of course, a different kettle of fish if you have plans to breed at any time in the future. You will inevitably choose a queen, as an unneutered tom in the home is seldom a success. Unneutered toms spray around the house, and will continue to do so until they have been neutered. If you don't want to breed, but would

like to show your Maine Coon, then the sex is again of little consequence. Both sexes, whether they are castrated or not, make good show cats. Because castrated toms and queens often have a better coat than uncastrated cats, they have show classes of their own.

A Kitten

If you already have other cats in the home, it will take a little longer for the new cat to get accustomed. In practice, a kitten will settle in more quickly than an adult cat. The most important factor in this kind of situation is your own patience and calmness and the way in which you introduce the newcomer. You know your own cats best

Red silver tabby blotched kitten

and you may already have a fair idea of which will readily accept the newcomer and which are likely to be awkward. It is worth knowing that most adult cats have a sort of built-in "brake" when it comes to a kitten. So although they might start hissing, the kitten will never be seriously attacked, bitten, or scratched. A kitten that has been properly socialized by the breeder will in fact know that not all other cats will automatically respond in a friendly manner. There will often be other cats living in the breeder's home that sometimes lash out at playful kittens gamboling past. A new kitten will usually have gotten used to his new home and his new housemates within a week or two. Whether or not the new cats become close pals or merely tolerate each other is hard to predict beforehand. Just like people, it's all a matter of personal preference.

Kittens are usually accepted without any problem

Another Adult Maine Coon

Introducing an adult into a group of cats demands more time and patience on the part of the owner. More often than is the case with kittens, the other cats will look upon the strange, adult animal as an intruder. So initially the owner will need to keep a close eye on the situation. The owner will also have to be able to cope with skirmishes. However, an adult Maine Coon that had no problems socializing with the cats of his previous owner, will not usually give rise to permanent problems at his new address either. Although it will generally take longer for an adult cat to settle than a kitten, things will almost always work out eventually.

Your Maine Coon and your Dog

Introducing a cat into a household that is already home to one or more dogs requires a different kind of knowledge and preparation than introducing a new cat into an existing group of cats. If you have dogs, and are considering buying a kitten, ask the (breed) association whether or not there are any litters available that have grown up with one or more dogs. Many breeders specify such as additional information in their advertisement or association registration. A kitten that is already accustomed to dogs will not easily get upset if a dog gets a bit rough with it. But properly socialized kittens that have not grown up with dogs can also adjust to dogs. Whether or not things work out will not only depend on the cat of course, the dog's attitude is equally important.

If your dog is used to cats, then you will be able to anticipate how it will react and allow for that during the introduction period. If your dog is not used to cats, then your first worry should not be the kitten but your dog. You must make it quite clear to your dog that it has to be very gentle with the kitten. However well the introduction seems to be going initially, you must always make sure that the kitten has a means of escape, for example, onto a sofa or cupboard, in case it suddenly gets scared. Obviously the dog should not be able to get to this "refuge." Reward your dog to help him understand that the kitten is something positive. If your dog walks past the kitten calmly or comes to you while the kitten is sit-

Black silver tabby kitten

Kittens that were raised without dogs around them can get used to dogs too

ting on your lap, for instance, reward him with a treat. He will soon associate the kitten with something positive. Last, but by no means least, never leave your dog and the new cat alone together at this stage. You should not do that until you are absolutely certain that they are well acquainted and accustomed to each other. That point has not been reached until the critical distance between them has been reduced to a minimum and their behavior towards each other is friendly.

The Maine Coon and Children

A Maine Coon is a family pet that enjoys human company, including that of children. To children, having a new pet in the home is quite a happening. Parents often buy a pet in the belief that it will be good for the children's development. It will teach them how to behave with animals and what it means to be jointly responsible for something. But a cat should never be bought simply "for the children." The final responsibility will of course lie with the adults in the home. Children will have to be taught that a cat or kitten is not a plaything that can be picked up and dragged around at whim. Teach your child that a cat—and especially a kitten!—has set sleeping times when it needs to be left in peace. Mind that the children are not overenthusiastic or boisterous with it. Teach them

how to pick a cat up safely, and explain that there are certain places–the basket, litter box, food bowl, and scratch post–where it should be left alone and not disturbed. It is a good idea to involve the children in the daily care of the cat, like feeding and grooming. That way they will learn that daily routine now has to accommodate the new housemate and that the cat has its own needs that have to be taken into account.

More than One Cat?

If your Maine Coon is your first pet, ask yourself whether or not a single cat would be best in your circumstances. Cats are not pack animals as such, like dogs, but they are most certainly sociable animals that want to, and indeed have the need to live in interaction with other cats and humans. At some stage–usually between about nine and sixteen weeks–the mother cat will make it quite clear to her kittens that its time for them to "fend for themselves." But that doesn't mean that the domestic cat, as we have known it now for more than seven thousand years, lives in solitude. Most cats, whether living on a farm, in a family home, or on a residential estate live together with other cats in the immediate vicinity. If a cat has been properly socialized, it will consider its human caregiver as its "mother cat superior." The human will fulfill the caring and feeding task, the mother cat used to fulfill (in the cat's perception, stroking is the same as cleaning). If you are away from home a lot of the time, due to full-time work or for another reason perhaps, it could be kinder to the kitten if you bought two cats at once. If you don't have much time to spend playing with your new kitten, another kitten as a playmate is very important to the kitten's mental well-

*Maine Coon
queen, bluecream
with white*

being. That is why many breeders refuse to part with a kitten if they know it is to be a lone pet in a household where the owner will be away a lot of the time.

Outdoor or Indoor Cat?

Although Maine Coons used to freely roam the farmyards in the industrialized and overpopulated areas we live in today, such relatively safe surroundings are often hard to find. Besides the dangers of busy traffic, cats also run the risk of getting lost or even stolen. Moreover, cats allowed to stay out also face health risks: various illnesses, some of them fatal, can be transmitted as a result of fighting, mating, or even just rubbing noses. A cat roaming freely outdoors can also come into contact with pesticides by eating

*If you are away
a lot, it would
be better to have
two kittens*

*Young Maine Coons
are no different
than
other breeds,
when it comes
to curiosity*

a poisoned mouse or rat, or can themselves be poisoned by eating food put out for them by cat haters. Last, but not least, a "free-range" cat can cause considerable social problems with your neighbors. There is nothing that ruins good neighborly relations as much as a cat that leaves its fences in someone else's garden or prowls around neighbors' aviaries and fishponds, not to mention sleep disturbed by noisy cats in nocturnal combat. You will notice that the breeder that sold you your cat will not allow his cats to roam freely outdoors. He or she will want the cats to live as safe and healthy a life as possible. There are plenty of alternatives that still enable you to let your cat get some fresh air, like fencing off your balcony or building a safe outdoor run. It is also often possible to fix special cat wire on top of garden fencing. It is a good idea to fit a catflap in the door leading into the fenced-off garden, to save you from having to play doorman all the time.

*A cat run is
a safe solution*

A Maine Coon's happiness does not actually depend on free access to a garden, but if you choose to keep your cat indoors, make sure it has plenty of playthings and climbing facilities, like a climbing frame or a sturdy scratch post. Ensure that screens have been properly fixed to all the windows, especially upstairs. Beware of some bottom-hung, top-opening windows. Even if the window is open at its widest, the cat will not usually be able to get out, which might give you a (false) sense of security. Several cats a year still try and end up getting stuck—with disastrous consequences.

A balcony can easily be fenced off

4 Buying a Maine Coon

The Pedigree as Proof of Authenticity

The fact that the Maine Coon, with its gentle character and robust appearance, has become immensely popular in recent years does have some drawbacks. The flip side of the coin will become clear to you when you decide to buy a kitten. Unfortunately, there are breeders you would be best

*Longhaired
domestic cats like
these are sometimes
called "Maine Coon
without a pedigree"*

not to buy from. You should be cautions if you come across an advertisement offering kittens without a pedigree because every purebred Maine Coon should have a pedigree! As the pedigree only represents a fraction of the Kitten's price, there is not a single legitimate reason why it should not be offered. Anybody who has a litter from two Maine Coons with pedigree can apply for a pedigree. Kittens without a pedigree, offered as "Maine Coon" or "Maine Coon cross" are usually nothing more than long-haired moggies of doubtful origin that some disreputable owner is hoping to get rich on. Should a kitten you have bought from that kind of breeder develop any health problems, you will have no grounds for any kind of claim from either the "breeder" or the breed association. No breed association will object to issuing a pedigree provided the breeder complies with certain basic requirements. These basic requirements relate, in particular, to prior testing for fatal viral illnesses and to a limit on the number of litters a cat may have within a certain period of time–the latter in the interests of the queen's health. In a nutshell, you can be fairly sure that there is something decidedly wrong with litters offered for sale without a pedigree.

A show winner in the bud? No breeder will be able to guarantee that

Buying a Kitten

Whether you want to keep a Maine Coon kitten simply as a family pet, or are contemplating breeding or showing your cat at a later stage, one thing is vital: Never simply buy a kitten from the first breeder you happen to come across. It makes good sense to learn more about the breed first, to read about it and to talk to breed enthusiasts. Cat and breed associations will be able to give you the names of breeders that currently have litters available. If you want a kitten and are considering breeding or showing it later, it is important that the kitten is not only cute and healthy, but also that it complies with the show standard. You should only ever buy a kitten from a reputable breeder who will be quite happy to tell you everything about the family lines your kitten comes from. He or she will be able to advise you on breeding and will be prepared to

They are all equally adorable, but an experienced breeder will spot the good and bad points regarding their appearance

help you learn how. Because you want to use your cat for breeding, it is also vital that the breeder has had his or her breeding stock tested for possible hereditary problems, and tells you of such openly and honestly. Of course, no breeder can guarantee that the promising little kitten you have just bought will turn out to be a show winner. Nobody can predict quite how a cat will develop, as that depends on so many things. If you do not intend to breed

Cream striped tom, four and a half months old

or show your cat, it is equally important that you buy your kitten from a serious, loving breeder who monitors character and hereditary health, but slight imperfections in terms of appearance need not be quite such an issue. The kitten itself will not be in the slightest bit bothered if his ears are slightly off center, his head not quite perfectly shaped or his tail has a slight kink in it. In an average litter of four kittens, there will usually be only one or two that the breeder considers "good enough" (to be sold) for breeding. The rest of the litter will, of course, have had the same loving start and care as those one or two "top kittens." Moreover, the differences will sometimes be so minor that it would take an expert to spot them. If there is any kind of "defect," such as an umbilical hernia or a kink in the tail, that the breeder may consider undesirable in view of the possibility of inheritance, it is quite possible that he or she will ask you to sign a purchase agreement in which you promise never to use the cat for breeding purposes. This will help the breeder to exclude weaknesses from the breed in the future.

Red tabby with a white kitten, four weeks old

Choosing a Kitten

Once you have decided to bring a Maine Coon kitten into your home, the cat or breed association will be able to give you telephone numbers of breeders with available litters.

Two white tom kittens; their characters might make one of them more appealing to you than the other

The first contact is usually made by telephone, after which you will visit the breeder. He or she may have just the one queen with a litter, but could also have a large group with several queens and possibly one or more stud toms in separate runs or pens. However, if the house you are invited into appears to be overrun with cats and/or you notice that the animals there do not seem to be part of the family, then it is not a good sign. Every cat needs individual care and attention, and that is simply impossible in such large numbers. There might well be several litters, but even then the kittens should be raised in the home, with the other cats and people. There is no excuse for leaving a kitten in a separate room or (outside) run to

Page 41
By the time you get your kitten home, he is past that fluffy-ball stage

grow up far from any attention or social interaction. All being well, you should be welcomed by a serious breeder who will give you the impression that he or she breeds with love and attention for each animal. The breeder will not usually invite you to see the kittens until they are

about four weeks old. This is because it is hard to say much about the individual character of very young kittens. Their behavior and appearance cannot really be assessed until they start moving around the house independently and start to eat. When you go to visit the kittens, observe whether they are open to people do they move around the living room freely? Do they scare easily? A well-socialized kitten will usually love visitors, and before you know it you will have several of them climbing up your trouser leg and onto the sofa to say hello. Make a point of noticing whether or not the house is clean. Your nose will probably tell you if there is a spraying tom in the house (the smell permeates everything), but the litter boxes should certainly be kept clean and the kittens should appear well looked after and healthy. The kittens shouldn't have any discharge in their eyes or show any symptoms of disease, and their coat should be clean and free of bald patches. The queen will have been feeding her kittens for some time now, which will have taken its toll on her physical condition. So she could well look a little skinny and somewhat "out-of-coat." Despite this though, her eyes should still be bright and she should be calm, loving, and not mind visitors handling her young. Do not make an appointment with more than one breeder on the same day. The animals at one address might have health problems and you could unintentionally transmit the pathogenic bacteria from one breeder to the other on your clothes or skin.

Page 42
Golden tabby
queen

Why Choose that Particular Kitten?

The most important factor to consider when choosing your new housemate is that the kitten is healthy and has a character that appeals to you. After all, you hope to have a healthy, affectionate, and problem-free pet for years to come and a good start is essential. As far as the character is concerned, trust your own instinct. If you happen to take to a particular kitten because of something it does, then there is nothing to stop you from choosing that kitten. If you intend to show or breed the cat later, an experienced breeder will be able to tell you whether or not the kitten has what it takes. But no matter which kitten you fall for, you should never make any concessions as far as health is concerned. An unethical breeder may try to sell you a pitiful "runt" for less than the full price. You are advised to resist the temptation, as more often than not there will be something wrong with it. Resisting the temptation now could save you a lot of upset, worry, and high veterinary bills later.

Page 45
Black tortie
silver tabby queen

Young, black
and white tom

Taking your Kitten Home

A serious breeder will want to pass the kittens on to you when they are about thirteen weeks old, as the kitten will not have been fully vaccinated against feline influenza and other such diseases until then. This is usually done at the age of two and three months so optimum immunity will have been reached by the fourteenth week. The kitten will have been wormed several times. Experience also shows that a kitten will not be able to fend for itself socially until about that age. If you reserved your kitten at an early age, it might be possible for you to visit it a couple of times to see how it is growing and developing. A serious breeder will have no objection to that. He or she will appreciate your interest and will take the time to answer any questions you have and to offer advice during such visits as well. A breeder will often prefer to personally deliver the kitten to its new owner. It can make it easier for the kitten to settle in his new environment if there's someone familiar with it during the move, and at the same time the breeder will be able to see where his/her kitten will be living. You will usually receive the pedigree and vaccination certificate at the same time, but sometimes the pedigree is forwarded later. It is common practice to pay the full agreed price when the ownership is transferred, deducting any advance deposit paid when the kitten was reserved. Some breeders draw up a purchase agreement specifying the rights and obligations of the breeder (seller) and the new owner (buyer). You are advised to read any such contract carefully to check that the contents are what you had agreed and expected.

Travel basket

Never transport your Maine Coon loose in the car or in a harness on your lap. A strong travel basket like this one is the safest means of transport for your cat and will cause it the least amount of stress.

5 FEEDING

Shop-bought or Homemade?

The shops are full of a wide range of dried and canned cat food. Some people, nevertheless, prefer to prepare their own. If you choose to prepare your cat's main food yourself, you must make sure that it contains all the nutrients it needs and in the right proportions. Feeding your cat on fish alone, or on nothing but liver could cause problems, for example, because such an unbalanced diet lacks certain essential nutrients and could be detrimental to your cat's health in the long term. Most people, therefore, choose to buy commercially produced cat food as a staple diet, so that they can be sure that their pet is getting all the necessary nourishment. In addition, there is a wide variety of fresh foods you can feed your cat, such as boiled lamb or lamb's heart, boiled fish (fillets), boiled chicken or turkey, and game. Fresh meat or fresh fish is best not given raw because there is a risk of bacterial contamination. You are particularly advised not to feed your cat raw "high-risk meat," which includes chicken. Some people only ever feed their cats day-old chicks, available frozen from pet stores. The composition of day-old chicks is very similar to that of the natural prey of small members of the cat family. Day-old chicks and pieces of meat are also good for the teeth, it force the cat to use its premolars and helps to prevent tartar buildup and the dental problems that can cause.

Does Cheap Become Expensive?

A cat is a carnivore, which means that it has a short gastrointestinal tract that can only digest high-quality animal proteins. Digesting lower quality vegetable proteins is much harder for a cat and will also deliver much less nourishment. Good, commercially produced food should, therefore, contain a high proportion of animal proteins and fats. It is quite simply a matter of paying for quality; most of the more expensive brands primarily contain animal proteins and fats, whereas the manufacturers of cheaper brands tend to use more vegetable proteins as a cheap "filling." If you want to keep your cat fit and healthy in the long term, then cheap always ends up being expensive. Quality, which means better cat food, be it dried or canned, with prime ingredients and good sources

of animal protein will keep your cat fit and healthy for longer than a cheap food that contains too much waste and vegetable protein. If you use dried food, take note of the production and use-by dates. Depending on the kinds of preservative used, food of which the shelf life has been exceeded can sometimes become toxic. The fats in them can turn rancid, which can irrevocably damage the liver, and be fatal in the worst scenario.

How Much and How Often?

The Maine Coon might be the largest breed of cat, but that doesn't automatically mean it has the largest appetite. The food requirement will vary per cat, influenced by factors such as age, level of activity, metabolism and whether or not the cat has been neutered. Once a Maine Coon has reached adulthood, it will not eat more than an average, smaller breed. It is, nevertheless, essential that each cat be given the quantity and sort of food that specifically suits his or her situation. A queen still feeding a litter of kittens will obviously require more food, and of a different quality than a spayed cat. How often a cat is fed will also depend on the situation. A growing and highly active Maine Coon kitten will need several, relatively small meals a day, whilst one or two concentrated meals a day will be sufficient for a castrated cat.

Water

The same applies for every single cat; the only good and suitable drink for a cat is clean water. So make sure that there are always bowls of fresh water ready for your cat, preferably in several different places throughut the house. Refresh the water daily.

Sweets and Treats

Various brands of cat sweets are marketed today. The question, however, is whether or not they should be given to cats at all. A cat does not need rewarding for a correctly executed exercise the way a dog does, and it can encourage unwanted begging. Cat sweets do not contain extra ingredients that are essential for the cat's health, everything he needs is already in the meals he gets.

Grass is essential to help a cat get rid of hairballs

Furthermore, cat sweets can actually be damaging to the health if too many are given too often. Properly fed cats, for example, already get their daily portion of vitamin A, a vitamin that cats cannot excrete. But the vitamin is also in cat sweets and if the cat is given more than one or two a day, health problems are to be expected. If you want to give your cat a special treat every now and then, it would be better to give it a little sterilized cream (sterilizing the cream breaks down the lactose), or a thin slice of roast beef or salmon.

Hairballs

Because of its long coat, a Maine Coon can occasionally suffer from hairballs. Cats have little barbs, or hooks, on their tongues facing backwards, towards the throat. Any hairs that get caught on the tongue are therefore very difficult, if not impossible to spit out, and end up disappearing into the stomach. They then form a hairball that the cat, from time to time, will regurgitate. Grass can aid the

By playing with your cat a lot, you will stop it from getting too fat

process, but if your cat does not have access to grass outdoors, a tray of special cat grass could be a useful alternative to help bring up the hairballs. Be careful that your cat does not start eating your houseplants–some can be very poisonous.

Large is Not Necessarily Fat

Cats are no different than humans, in that a fat cat is not a healthy cat. There will be too much unnecessary strain on the heart, liver and kidneys, so that the cat will feel unwell, and become lethargic and underactive. This becomes a vicious circle because lack of exercise will convert the excess of calories into fat more quickly. In addition, for a large breed of cat like the Maine Coon with its heavy bone structure, excess strain on the joints (particularly the knees and hips) can cause serious damage. It can lead to arthritis, which in the worst case can only be treated operatively. If a cat is too fat, the owner should consider the animal's actual daily food requirement and adjust the

Blue striped tom

quantity and type of food the cat is fed accordingly. A vet's advice could be sought to compile a diet plan so that the cat can gradually lose weight until the target weight has been reached. Moreover, extra treats should be cut out altogether and the now lazy gastrointestinal system should be stimulated by feeding at one or two fixed

Tasty is not necessarily the same as healthy, when it comes to cat food

A seven-year old castrated cat, not too fat, and not too thin

If your cat drinks out of the fish bowl or flower vase, change the water regularly

times a day. A cat that needs to lose weight should not be allowed to eat at random, so don't leave a bowl of dried food down all day. It is also a good idea if the owner plays with the cat for a while at set times, preferably before feeding, to simulate a "hunt the prey" situation. This combines weight loss with a better physical condition.

Silos like this one are useful if you keep a large group of cats

Cats Should Never Fast

Fat cats should never be allowed to fast. Fats will get into the blood system as a result of fasting, and be deposited in the liver. This will eventually lead to fatty degeneration of the liver and, ultimately, liver failure. So if your cat is overweight, it is best to switch to a low-calorie food and encourage it to get more exercise.

6 CARING FOR YOUR CAT

The Coat

One look at a Maine Coon's coat and you know that this is a cat built to survive a harsh, cold climate. Its shining coat

Cats look after their own coats - but occasional help is welcome

is closely implanted and will withstand a good deal of rain. Yet despite its being so thick, the coat does not get tangled very easily, thank goodness. That means that grooming can be limited to a thorough brushing every couple of days and checking and combing the areas where the coat is more prone to tangle (armpits, groins and the "'breeches" under the tail). The tail, thick and bushy as it is, should not be forgotten either. In the Maine Coon there is a clear difference between the long, full, thick winter coat and the much lighter, sometimes even very short, summer coat. The winter coat will, therefore, require more grooming than the summer coat. During

Cat brush

molting, when the coat is changing, the dead hair will have to be brushed out more often. This is especially necessary during the transition from thick winter coat to the much thinner summer coat. You can even pull whole tufts of hair out carefully between your thumb and finger. If you groom your Maine Coon properly, it will not swallow very much hair when it licks

White odd-eyed kitten

and washes itself. Sometimes though, a hairball can still form in the stomach that, in serious cases, has to be removed operatively. A special paste is available from vets for cats that frequently suffer from hairballs. The paste makes, the hairballs fall apart so that they can be digested and discharged naturally.

Washing

It is really only ever necessary to wash a Maine Coon if it has gotten particularly dirty. You should preferably use a gentle shampoo, such as baby shampoo or a special cat shampoo. If your pet is used to a running tap, a shower spray, or standing in the bath or shower cubicle, then it will usually not be scared of being washed occasionally. Some cats want nothing of it though, and for them there are special dry powder or bran shampoos on the market. These can be rubbed into a dry coat. The fat and dirt that has accumulated in the excreted skin fat is absorbed by the powder or bran. Once the dry shampoo has been rubbed into the coat well, the excess of skin fat and the dirt can be brushed out together. The result of such beauty treatment is a clean, fresh, and bouncy coat.

Preparing for a Show

If you plan to take your Maine Coon to a show, then grooming it thoroughly will be absolutely essential. Brushing alone will not always be sufficient, sometimes the cat will need to be washed first. A cat looking as if it battled through a forest to get to the show will obviously be awarded fewer points than an equally attractive cat that does have a clean coat. A cat show is a beauty contest, after all. Your cat's breeder will be able to explain exactly how best to prepare your cat for a show and whether or not it will need washing first. This is because he or she will know the exact coloring and texture of your cat's coat and will have experience preparing cats for shows. If the cat is to be washed beforehand, this is best done a few days before the show, allowing the sebum production to be restored. Special color shampoos are on sale for some specific coat colors. Your cat's breeder will usually know from experience which would be the best to use. The nails of any cat to be showed must always be trimmed.

Different Sorts of Coat

Every coat has its own structure, depending on things like the color and pattern. That is why not every coat can be cared for in the same way. This shaded puss' coat, for example, will require a different approach to the firmer coat of a black tabby – certainly if the cat is to be showed, advice from the breeder in this respect would be most welcome.

Young white tom

Stainless steel bowls are more hygienic than plastic ones

Stud tail and feline acne

Hormonal changes in adult toms, and sometimes in queens, can cause the sebaceous glands to become overactive, resulting in an excessive production of sebum at the base of the tail (the condition known as 'stud tail') and on the bottom of the chin ('feline acne'). An untreated stud tail will lead to hair loss in the affected area and the pores can become blocked and inflamed. Characteristic of feline acne are black spots around the chin that can also become inflamed. This can be avoided if the skin is soothed with something like calendula cream. Severe inflammations may need antibiotic treatment. Extra vitamin B, and food with a high content of prime animal fat, can help prevent the problem recurring. The problem will usually disappear altogether if the cat is castrated.

If your cat suffers from feline acne, it could help to replace any plastic feeding bowls with metal or glazed earthenware ones. However often or well you wash plastic bowls, traces of bacteria still remain, with a constant risk of reinfection and recurrent inflammation.

The Purpose of a Scratch Post

Any cat, and especially the Maine Coon with its sturdy legs and strong nails, will sharpen its nails by scratching. However, your furniture, doorpost, wallpaper and carpets do not have to suffer for it, provided you give your cat ample opportunity to scratch on something else. A strong scratch post or, better still, a robust, floor-to-ceiling climbing frame, if you have room for one, would be ideal. Make sure that the post or frame is high enough. If the cat stands on its back legs and stretches out completely, it should still have enough space left to stretch and scratch its front paws. Many standard scratch posts will be too small for a Maine Coon, and sometimes they won't be stable enough either. From day one, it is of course up to you to teach your kitten that it may not sharpen its nails on anything other than its scratch post or climbing frame. Once a cat has gotten used to scratching on other objects as well, it will be much harder to break the habit. If the cat starts scratching on something it shouldn't, pick it up and put it down again in the scratching position against the scratch post or frame. Contrary to popular belief, scratching is not only a means of sharpening the nails and keeping them short. Cats have scent glands on the back of their paws that secrete a scent humans cannot smell. So scratching is also a way of "leaving a card," saying as much as "I live here" or "this is mine." If your cat persists in scratching in the same places in the house, there is a way of breaking the habit. Rub a cloth over the side of your cat's head (it has identical scent glands near its temples) and then rub the cloth over the places your cat likes to scratch. If your cat walks past the treated spot, it will recognize its own scent and think it has already "done" that spot.

A good scratching post is no luxury

Clipping a Cat's Nails

Although sufficient scratching will usually keep the nails trimmed and stop them from growing too long, it does-n't always wear them down sufficiently. This is particular-ly the case in cats that never go outdoors. The nail tips can become too long and razor-sharp, and your cat can get caught in the furniture or hurt itself when it jumps off your lap and gets caught in your clothes. Sharp nail tips are best removed occasionally with good, sharp nail clip-pers. Be careful to cut the tips only though, if you cut too far you will cut into "life" and cause unnecessary bleed-ing. Any queen going to a stud for mating and any cat going to a show should always have clipped nails. If you start clipping its nails when your kitten is still quite young, it will soon get used to it and won't protest too much later.

Nail clippers

Ears

Although the Maine Coon has fairly large and open ears, he seldom has any trouble with them. There are enough protective hairs on the inside to prevent dirt and dust from getting in. Some cats have an excess of wax in the inner ear. Never try to remove this with cotton buds. That merely pushes the dirt further into the ear and can cause inflammations. Buy a bottle of special feline eardrops. Once the drops have soaked in, you can gently remove the softened dirt with a tissue. You can also use a soft cotton bud, provided you don't push it into the auditory duct. Another problem you could face is ear mite, an extremely infectious parasite that will need veterinary treatment.

Symptomatic of ear mites are constantly dirty ears. A cat with ear mites will have a dark brown, sticky, gritty discharge coming out of its ears, no matter how well you clean them. Medication against ear mite sometimes has to be given for a long time. Because ear mite is contagious, you will also have to check and, if necessary, treat any other cats (and dogs) in the house.

Eyes

A Maine Coon's eyes need little looking after. The mod-

Maine Coons seldom have trouble with their ears

erate shape of the head gives little reason to expect chronic blockages. If your cat has inflamed eyes, an infection will always be the cause and it will be up to your vet to decide how best to treat it. Never attempt self-medication where inflamed eyes are concerned. The eyes are sensitive and susceptible and there is a wide diversity of possible causes. An eye infection can sometimes be caused by a blocked tear duct, so that the eye fluid can no longer be discharged through the nose and therefore keeps "leaking" along the lower lid. In that case, the vet will try to "prick through" the tear duct with a minute flexible tube—this is a minor operation.

Black blotched
tom

Teeth

Just like people, cats start out with milk teeth and grow second, permanent teeth. A kitten will lose its milk teeth between the ages of four and six months. The process will usually go unnoticed, because a cat's new tooth usually comes through as soon as the milk tooth has fallen out. Sometimes the new tooth will already be visible behind the milk tooth and it will push the milk tooth out so that it almost looks as if there aren't any new teeth at all. Occasionally, a milk eyetooth does not fall out, causing the permanent tooth to grow crooked. If that is the case, the vet will usually extract the milk tooth. So it is a good idea to examine your kitten's teeth regularly between the ages of four and six months. Just like people, cats are also susceptible to cavitries, tartar, and gingivitis. Thanks to the prolonged life expectancy, and the ready-made food that cats hardly have to sink their teeth into, dental problems in older cats are commonplace. This can lead to chronic pain, inflammations, loss of appetite, and eventual loss of teeth. Make a habit of regularly checking your cat's teeth for tartar and inflammations. If necessary, the vet can remove the tartar, extract the affected tooth and treat any inflammations with antibiotics. Some family lines of van Maine Coons are especially susceptible to dental problems, seen not only in older animals, but also some younger cats with serious dental trouble. If this is the case with your cat, report it to the breeder so that he or she can take this into account when breeding.

Fleas

Even cats that never go outdoors can get fleas. You, your visitors, or you dog can bring them into the home. If your cat starts scratching excessively and you find dark granules (flea excrement) when you spread the coat on his back, near the tail, then you know it's time for action. Fleas are harmful to your pet's health. Not only because they drink its blood, but also because they can transmit tapeworm infections. If a cat with fleas is left untreated, the fleas will multiply incredibly fast. If you're not careful your house will be infested with fleas within a matter of

Kittens lose their milk teeth at between 4 and 6 months

*Fleas can be
a pest and are
not always
easy to combat*

Flea comb

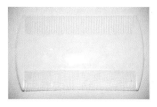

weeks, especially during hot and humid weather. Only ever buy approved pesticides from your vet, as he will only stock the best. To treat fleas effectively, you will not only have to treat the animal but also its environment.

The cat itself can be treated with a flea growth inhibitor in the form of a tablet, an ampoule, or drops in the neck. These products make fleas sterile, so that the countless eggs they produce will not hatch. However, you will also have to treat your pet's environment (i.e. your house) with an aerosol or spray to kill any and all fleas, eggs, and larvae floating about. Be careful when treating pregnant queens and kittens. Most products are not harmless. In principle, the only products that are safe are those, given

*Black silver
blotched queen
with white*

internally, based on the active ingredient lufenuron–but always read the guidelines on the pack or information sheet and, if you are in any doubt at all, contact either your vet or the manufacturer directly. Kittens with a bad case of fleas must always be taken seriously as the bugs can cause them to become anemic. Very severe cases left untreated can even be fatal. Again, it is better to consult a veterinary surgeon rather than doctoring with household remedies that could be very harmful to tender young kittens.

Worms

Worm infections are caused by roundworms, hookworms, or tapeworms. All these parasites can cause serious damage to the cat's organs. The mother of your Maine Coon kitten will normally have been wormed before mat-

Out in the grass, your cat could acquire worm eggs

ing and the breeder will have wormed your kitten several times. Worming treatment should be repeated once the kitten is six months old, and annually from then on. Good worming treatment can be obtained from the veterinarian, who will always have the latest generation of worm pastes and tablets in stock.

Your Cat in Heat

The average Maine Coon queen will come into heat for the first time when she is between five and twelve months old. She will remain into heat for three to ten days, will be

Spaying your queen is the only option if you don't want a litter

more affectionate, and will often make more noise than normal. If she is stroked she will lower her front legs, raising her posterior. She will keep rubbing her head against furniture, people, and other animals, and she will roll on the ground. This behavior will be alternated with long periods of rest and sleep. While a cat is in heat, she will often have less appetite than usual.

The periods between seasons can vary per cat. Some are in heat more intensely and for longer than others, and for some the interval between two seasons can be much longer than for others. Factors such as the days lengthening, warmth, and the presence of an unneutered tom in the vicinity, can all stimulate a queen to come into heat.

Spaying a Queen

If you do not intend to let your Maine Coon queen have a litter of kittens, it would be best to have your vet spay her. If you don't, continually being in heat can cause cysts in the uterus. It could also lead to inflammation of the uterus and possibly cancer later, particularly tumors in the mammary glands. The vet spays the queen, under general anesthetic, by removing the fallopian tubes, the ovaries, and the womb. As the hormone producing organs have been removed, the cat will no longer come in heat. Spaying is best done when the cat is fully grown, usually from the age of about eight months. If you are not yet certain whether or not you want to breed with your cat, you could put her on the cat pill. This will temporarily stop her coming into heat. Once you decide to mate her, stop the pill so that she will come into heat again. Don't take too long deciding though; the older a queen is when she has her first litter, the higher the risk of complications.

Castrating a Tom

A Maine Coon tom reaches adulthood between five and twelve months of age. He will then be capable of mating with and fertilizing a queen. His fertility and the willingness to mate is not limited to any particular period, toms

Once a tom has been neutered, he will be quieter and less inclined to roam

don't come into heat the way queens do. Many sexually mature toms start marking their environment. They do that by spraying a urine that has a strong and unpleasant musky scent.

This is why most toms, unless they are going to be used for breeding, are castrated before their first birthday. But their unpleasant habit of spraying is not the only thing that makes unneutered, potent toms unpleasant house-mates. As their hormone levels rise, so too does the tendency to roam and/or fight. Castration will usually put an end to these characteristics of sexual maturity, although it can take some time for all of them to disappear as the hormones that cause them leave the body only gradually.

Page 68
Young Maine Coon queen, black tortie silver blotched with white

Cat Tray and Litter

Your Maine Coon kitten will already have been house trained by the breeder but it will certainly take a little while to acclimatize to the new situation in your home. So to start with, here is some good advice: use the same cat litter the kitten was used to at the breeder's. Later–and gradually if possible–you can change to a different litter if you prefer.

The various kinds of litter all have their advantages and disadvantages. The clumping sorts of litter are the cheapest, available in both a fine and a coarse grain. If you use the cheaper sort of litter, it is important to fill the tray because the clumps will otherwise stick to the bottom of the tray and be more difficult to remove. Other sorts are made from compressed paper, wood fiber or maize waste. The latter is also a clumping litter, making easy to scoop out. Cat trays are available in all shapes and sizes. Make sure the one you choose for your Maine Coon is big enough, the bigger the better, in fact. A hood on the tray will prevent the cat from spilling litter over the edges while it is raking over its feces.

Choose a place (or places, if you have more than one tray) where the kitten will feel safe and protected, especially if there are other cats in the house. As kittens only have little bladders, it is a good idea to have a cat tray in the living room as well to start with.

Cat Trays and Hygiene Practice

In the interests of everybody's health, it is important that you observe good hygiene practice regarding the cat tray. To avoid disease, it is essential that the clumps are scooped

out every day, or that the whole tray is cleaned if non-clumping litter is used. Particularly in hot summers, a cat tray is a breeding ground for bacteria and, therefore, a possible source of disease. Clean the entire tray at least twice a week, preferably using a good disinfectant like bleach. Good hygiene practice regarding cat trays is not only better for the cat's health, it can also help solve or prevent house-training problems.

If you have several cats, provide several cat trays in various places. Many cats prefer to urinate in one place and to mess in another. This is because urine is also used as a means of marking their territory whereas feces betray the cat's presence and are, therefore, instinctively buried. Remember not to put the litter tray too close to the cat's food or drinking bowls—no cat likes doing its business near its food. If, despite good hygiene and adequate litter trays, a cat still urinates in places you'd rather it didn't, as a result of insecurity or anxiety, a pheromone spray might help. They are available from specialist pet stores and veterinarians' offices.

Suddenly incontinent?

If a cat that is usually well house-trained suddenly seems incontinent, a health problem such as cystitis or late-onset diabetes could be the cause. If your cat suddenly becomes incontinent, always consult your vet before jumping to any conclusions.

Kittens

7 Abnormalities, Diseases and Other Problems

General

It would be impossible to discuss all feline diseases and abnormalities in this book. We have, therefore, decided to deal with a number of important diseases and abnormalities that you and your Maine Coon are likely to encounter sooner or later. The following problems can occur in all cats, regardless of the breed. However, individuals within a particular breed are related and, therefore share certain characteristics. This not only produces similar appearances, but can also cause certain hereditary health problems to occur more or less frequently within a particular breed population. Such problems tend to arise within a small section of a particular breed, and a serious breeder will do everything he can to minimize the risks. Among good Maine Coon breeders there is a strong sense of responsibility about breeding. Compared with some colleagues, they sometimes seem

*Maine Coons are
normally strong and
healthy cats*

Provided kittens are vaccinated in time, the risk of them catching feline distemper or cat flu is practically nil.

to assume a pioneering role in reducing hereditary problems, and that might give you the impression that Maine Coons are more susceptible to health problems than other breeds. This is not the case; generally speaking, the Maine Coon is a strong, healthy, and resilient cat. Having said that, any cat can fall ill at some stage in his or her life, no matter how carefully it was bred and looked after. If your cat becomes ill, the vet is obviously the first person you should consult, but it could also be worth contacting the breeder, who may be able to aid and advise as well.

Feline distemper and cat 'flu

Feline distemper is an extremely contagious disease that is almost always fatal. Feline distemper is caused by the panleukopenia virus and easily spread among cats. Cat 'flu is a collective term for various viruses, caused primarily by the feline calici virus and the feline rhinotracheitis virus. Effective vaccinations are available against both feline distemper and cat 'flu. Kittens are usually given a cocktail vaccination against both diseases at about two months and again at three months. This will help the kitten build up its own antibodies against the disease. The vaccination should be repeated every two to three years for feline distemper, and annually for cat flu. The cocktail component against feline distemper offers almost total protection. However, should a vaccinated cat come into contact with cat flu, it might still catch a cold. But it will certainly not be as ill as it would have been had it not been vaccinated, and it will not die because of the disease. Consult your veterinarian to discuss the best vaccination program for cat flu. That will depend on how many cats you have at home, and on whether or not you take them to shows or breed.

FIV

Feline aids, FIV, is a viral infection for which there is no vaccination, and it is always fatal in the long term. The viral infection is related to the AIDS virus in humans, but feline AIDS is not contagious to humans and human AIDS is not contagious to cats. The disease is transmitted predominantly through biting, and sometimes through mating. Very rarely, the virus can be transmitted at birth from the queen to her kittens. The virus can only spread if it is allowed to pass from an infected cat directly into the blood system of another cat. Feline AIDS is mostly trans-

Young black and white tom

mitted by uncastrated, roaming toms fighting to defend their territory. The course of the disease varies—whilst one cat might stay healthy for years, another will display typical symptoms quite quickly and die. Typical FIV symptoms are fever, diarrhea, weight loss and the formation of tumors. Because the virus causes a gradual decline in the cat's immune system, most sufferers eventually die from an infection that can no longer be cured. A simple veterinary blood test will ascertain whether or not a cat is FIV positive. Cat breeders always have all their stud animals tested for FIV. Your carefully bred Maine Coon kitten will, therefore, be free of the virus when you take it home. There is no cure for FIV. The medications that can be prescribed are expensive equivalents to the medications given to humans to slow down the systemic damage caused by AIDS. Such treatment for cats is still in an experimental phase, however. Ensuring that your cat cannot contract FIV is, therefore, the most important measure, and that means that you must avoid your cat being able to come into contact with other cats that might be infected. The best way of avoiding possible problems is not to allow your cat to roam freely outdoors, and to have a vet test any other cats you have for FIV before your new cat arrives.

Red silver tabby tom

Red and white young tom

Black and white queen

Black silver tabby and white queen

FeLV

Feline Leukemia Virus, FeLV, is a contagious and eventually fatal virus. It can be transmitted through excrements biting and licking, or by eating from the same bowl as an infected cat. As is the case with FIV, the virus affects the animal's immune system. One of the most common symptoms of FeLV is leukemia (blood cancer). Although there is a vaccination against FeLV, it is not administered on a wide scale. The level of protection the vaccination offers is not very high and it does not always prevent a vaccinated cat from getting leukemia. People that use their purebred cats for breeding prefer to have the vet do a blood test to be absolutely certain that their cats do not carry the virus. The same advice applies in respect of the leukemia virus: if you want to avoid your cat contracting it, do not let it roam around outdoors and have the blood of all other cats in the house, and any new cats, tested for antibodies against the virus before they arrive.

Bluecream
and white queen

FIP

Black silver
tabby kitten,
four weeks old

Feline Infectious Peritonitis is an acute inflammatory reaction of the body following exposure to certain corona viruses. Corona viruses are found in many animals and

are usually quite harmless. Very occasionally though, there can be a mutation of the viruses the cat has, resulting in a form the immune system is unable to combat. The cat can become ill, have a fever, a pot belly, or display other strange symptoms, and will not usually respond well to medication. Eventually, and sometimes after a brief respite, the cat will die. A definite diagnosis can only be made afterwards by post-mortem examination. Little is known about the cause, although it does seem that a genetic element might play a role. In a small percent of cats, this results in a "flawed" immune system, that responds wrongly to the mutant corona viruses, and the body destroys itself. If a cat has produced several offspring that have died of FIP, it is best not to use her for breeding anymore.

A litter of blue tabby kittens

Fungal infections

Fungus, or ringworm, is an awkward skin infection that is usually caused by the fungus Microsporum canis. A cat with ringworm will develop symptomatic bald patches, especially on the head. Left untreated, bald patches will also develop on other parts of the body. Ringworm can affect cats and humans and is transmitted by direct contact. There will also be spores all over the house and these can easily be carried on the skin and clothes. The infection can be treated with a combination of tablets (a six-week course of specific antibiotics) and can also be tackled with high doses of lufenuron. The house containing the fungus must also be disinfected several times to kill

Black blotched tom

*Black blotched
and white kitten*

off the spores. Ringworm is not life threatening, but is difficult to treat. If you use your animals for breeding and one of your cats has ringworm, then discontinue breeding until you have the problem under control. There is otherwise a large risk that you will pass the problem on to others.

Bladder stones

Because they have a longer urinary tract, toms are more susceptible to bladder stones than queens. If the acidic balance in the bladder is upset, tiny crystals can get left behind that, in time, can block the urethra. This makes it impossible for the cat to urinate and waste products will accumulate in the blood system and the rest of the cat's body. Without swift veterinary intervention, the cat could die of acute toxication. If the acidity in the bladder is too alkaline, "struvite" crystals will form. If it is too acid then "oxalate" crystals will form. It is important that the vet takes samples of the crystals and has them analyzed in a laboratory to determine which type they are. A special diet will be advised to prevent recurrence and the diet will depend on the type of crystal. Struvite crystals will gradually dissolve once the cat is fed the prescribed diet, whereas oxalite crystals will remain in the bladder once they have formed. If a large number of oxalite crystals have been detected, you will be advised to have them surgically removed before taking any dietary measures. Following the operation you can monitor the acidity of the urine with litmus to check that it stays within the normal limits.

Hypertrophic Cardiomyopathy

Hypertrophic Cardiomyopathy (HCM) is a hereditary heart condition. In cats suffering from HCM, the muscle of the left ventricle gradually thickens, so that it can no longer expand normally. Heart failure can follow, as can emboli (blood clots blocking a blood vessel), strokes or paralysis of the hindquarters. Early symptoms can be minor and, therefore, easily overlooked. The following complaints can occur: poor appetite, difficult breathing, tiredness, rapid breathing, heart murmur, and paralysis. A cat suffering from HCM can also appear to be perfectly healthy for a very long while and then suddenly die of cardiac arrest. Some cats have heart murmurs, others do not. It is difficult to predict whether a cat with HCM will become ill at an early age or later in life. Eventually though, a cat with HCM will die of heart failure. However, with a proper diagnosis, and the right medication–dilatants, diuretics, and medicines to regulate the heart function–a cat can live on for quite a long while

Kittens can't be tested for hereditary heart and kidney conditions, only adult cats can be tested.

with far fewer problems. The only way of diagnosing HCM is an ECG, done by a specialized radiologist using specific equipment called a color doppler. HCM is one of the most common heart conditions in cats and occurs in both purebreds and crossbred cats. The condition also occurs in Maine Coons so serious breeders have their cats tested. Because a tom's heart is not fully grown until the age of two, and a queen's heart not until she is three, it is not until then that a vet can be reasonably certain (80%) that a cat does not have HCM at that point in time. However, if tests prove positive, then the diagnosis is 100% certain. Breeders often have their queen undergo an indicative ultrasound scan before having a first litter. That way they can be sure that her heart will not fail in the straining period ahead during pregnancy, labor and feeding. To be on the safe side she will have another scan, when she is at least three years old. A tom used for breeding will be scanned several times during his life as well. This should preferably be done before he sires for the first time and then again, for safety's sake, several years later, sometimes years after he has been castrated. This is done to be as sure as possible that he doesn't have a problem that he could pass on to his offspring. HCM is inherited in cats as an autosomal dominant condition, which means that once an animal is affected, approximately half

Adult black blotched tom

of its offspring will have HCM. This also means that a cat with HCM will have at least one parent with HCM. For several years now, ultrasound scans have been carried out in an effort to reduce HCM in Maine Coons. The problem is expected to be under control within the next few years. Provided breeders only use the offspring of scanned parents to breed, and these new parents are also scanned at a later stage with good test results, then this need not be a pipe dream. You are therefore highly recommended to buy your kitten from a breeder who has had preventive testing carried out on his cats. That is your best guarantee that your cat will still have a healthy heart in old age.

A cat can be ill without it showing on the outside

PKD (Polycystic Kidney Disease)

PKD (Polycystic Kidney Disease) is a kidney condition that not only affects cats but also many other mammals, including humans. As a result of a hereditary error, cysts gradually form in the kidneys: pockets of fluid making it increasingly difficult for the kidneys to work as filters. An animal with PKD will eventually die of kidney failure. PKD is incurable and can only be temporarily relieved by a special diet to minimize the strain on the kidneys. There are various possible causes of renal failure. If you suspect any kidney problems, it is essential that you have a vet do

*Black tortie
striped queen*

a blood test that will measure the levels of waste products (creatinine and ureum). Any cat with premature kidney malfunction can be screened by echographic scanning to determine whether cysts are the cause. PKD is occasionally seen in Maine Coons. Breeders taking their cats to the radiologist to have their heart scanned for HCM, often ask for the kidneys to be screened at the same time. Kidney cysts cannot be identified under ten months. As with HCM, PKD is inherited as an autosomal dominant condition, which means that if a cat has inherited it, at least one of its parents will already have it, and half of its offspring will inherit it.

Hip Dysplasia

Hip Dysplasia (HD) is a partially hereditary condition caused by a combination of different genes and polygenes. The condition is common in dogs but also in cats.
The hip joints of a cat with HD become increasingly unstable because the "ball and socket" joint doesn't fit properly. This instability puts an abnormal strain on the

hip joint; friction between the elements makes all movement very painful and will eventually lead to arthritis. If a cat suffers from HD, the process will usually be gradual. Movement will become stiffer and increasingly difficult, the cat will sometimes appear to be in pain and will try to avoid running and jumping. It might suddenly not want to be picked up, or complain if it is touched. Contrary to dogs, problems really only arise in cats with a severe case of HD. Maine Coons are large animals, so their bones are under greater physical strain than smaller breeds, and the kitten usually grow quickly. The condition was consequently noticed within the breed, and breeders started to act proactively. By the year 2000, 513 X-rays of Maine Coons had been submitted to the International Research Institute (the OFA in the United States) for evaluation. 23% of these cases proved to be hip dysplasia. HD is partially hereditary; breeding with HD-negative stock only will help reduce the condition considerably. By having X-Rays done in accordance with the international guidelines issued by the OFA, and submitting the X-Rays to the institute for evaluation, a breeder can find out whether his or her cat has healthy hips. Test results are definite from the age of two – any test results

Black tortie and white queen

given before then are provisional as the cat will not be fully grown until it is two years old. Results specify a varying degree of HD – Excellent; Good; Fair; Borderline; Mild; Moderate or Severe. The evaluation of HD in cats is a developing field of knowledge. Other countries are expected to develop their own test criteria in the near future so that X-Rays will no longer have to be sent to the United States.

Patella Luxation

Loose kneecaps, or Patella Luxation (PL), are a hereditary condition seen in both dogs and cats. In severe cases the kneecap ('patella') is so loose that the cat has serious problems walking and jumping and the kneecap can easily dislocate. The cause is hereditary but Patella Luxation cannot be blamed on a single gen. The condition is "polygenic," i.e. several genes are responsible. Sometimes the patella is properly located in a well-formed groove, but the ligaments holding the joint together are too loose. Sometimes the knee joint itself is not properly formed, there might be too shallow a groove, for instance. Surgery will often be necessary in severe cases. The ligaments can be shortened, or the groove deepened so that the joint fits again properly. Breeders usually have their kittens and their stud cats manually tested for the condition. This is best done by a veterinarian or specialist with experience in assessing knee joints in cats. PL can be reduced easily by breeding with PL-negative stock only.

Deafness

Hereditary deafness is sometimes seen in all breeds of all-white cat, so that includes all-white Maine Coons. Deafness is one of the possible side effects of the dominant W gene, responsible for the lack of pigment in the hair, making the coat appear optically white. Contrary to what we can read in past literature, the color of the eyes is of no relevance; cats with two copper eyes, one copper and one blue eye (odd-eyed) or with two blue eyes can all be deaf in one or both ears. The chance of deafness in copper-eyed cats is nevertheless smaller. The cause of deafness is the deformation of the sensory hairs in the inner ear. These sensory hairs receive incoming sound signals and transmit them through the aural nerve to the brain. Deformed sensory hairs do not function properly.

White cats that are to be showed or used for breeding should be BEAR tested for deafness

Breeders of all-white Maine Coons will never cross two all-white cats, as this would increase the risk of deafness. They also have their white stud cats tested by a veterinary specialist, using what is known as the BAER test. Besides detecting total deafness, this test can also detect deafness in one ear, something that is very hard to detect without special equipment. Deaf cats must not be used for breeding. Because this has been done in the past, and because deaf cats can be found in or behind the pedigrees of present Maine Coons, ridding the breed of deafness is still an ongoing process. Breeding with white Maine Coons remains a matter of reading the pedigrees carefully, testing the stud cats and excluding from the breeding program any cats that produce deaf offspring, even if they hear perfectly well themselves.

Page 89
Polydactylism
is not only seen
in Maine Coons,
but in domestic
cats as well

Polydactylism

Polydactylism, having more toes than normal, is an abnormality seen in all kinds of mammal, including the cat. Polydactylism is inherited as a dominant condition. Specifically in the Maine Coon, a number of cats appeared to have extra toes on their front or back paws. Although the gene that causes polydactylism is neither deadly nor pathogenic, it is hard to regulate. If polydactyl cats are used for breeding, kittens could be born with far too many toes or rudimentary toes. This could create problems for the cats walking or getting their extra toes caught. That is why all coordinating pedigree associations and federations of all breeds of cat, and that obviously includes the Maine Coon, specify in their breed standards that there should be five toes on each front paw and four on each back paw. Polydactyl cats are disqualified from shows. However, some breeders find the quality quite charming and keep cats with "an extra toe." Breeders that use polydactyl cats for breeding will never cross two polydactyl animals, to minimize the risk of extremely polydactyl offspring. It is really quite simple to exclude this particular abnormality; cats that do not have extra toes, even if they stem from a polydactyl line, do not have the gene so cannot pass it on.

*Page 91
Black silver
blotched queen*

8 BREEDING MAINE COONS

General

Plenty of general books have already been written on breeding purebred cats and the entire process of mating and pregnancy, the birth and raising of kittens. This rather falls beyond the scope of a breed monograph. Instead, we will discuss a number of aspects you should consider if you want to breed a litter of Maine Coons.

Breeding requirements

The breeder of your queen will be able to help you find a suitable stud

If you want to use your Maine Coon queen for breeding, there are several important aspects to consider. Every litter of purebred kittens born, contributes to the future of that particular breed. That means that you must take great care in deciding whether or not your queen is suitable for breeding. First of all, you will have bought your cat from a well-reputed breeder, who will be willing to help and advise. The queen will come from well-bred

*A considerable
responsibility rests
on the breeder's
shoulders*

lines screened for hereditary conditions before breeding.
The breeder will have investigated whether or not the kitten would be suitable for breeding and is prepared to
show you the ropes. However, that same breeder will also
expect you to be prepared to approach breeding seriously,
and to gather information and insight into the stronger
and weaker points of the breed in general, and your own
Maine Coon queen in particular. This means that you will
have showed your cat so that she could be appraised by
a qualified judge and seen by other breeders. Stud toms
often go to shows as well so that you can see them 'in the
flesh'. If your breeder has the breed at heart, he or she will
be more than willing to take the time to help you find
a suitable tom for your queen, possibly using pedigree
comparisons to do so. When breeding Maine Coons, particular note is taken of the cat's general balance and the
shape of its head. The breed standard in chapter 2 has
more information about the requirements and faults.

Health and Character

A queen anyone wants to use for breeding must of course
have a loving and stable character, and be fit and healthy.
The necessary genetic tests should be done well before
mating, as should blood tests to make sure that she is both
FeLV and FIV negative. It is also advisable to have the vet-

erinarian give her a general examination: Is she fully grown in terms of bone structure, is her pelvis well-formed, are her kneecaps loose and is she fit? Again, well before the scheduled mating, she should have been vaccinated against feline distemper and cat flu, wormed and, if necessary, deflead. Aided by your breeder, your own perceptions, pedigree research and the advice of the breed association, you will have chosen a suitable tom to mate with your queen. Hopefully you will have a litter of healthy kittens nine weeks later. Maine Coon queens usually give birth quite easily and have fairly large litters.

A future breeding queen should have a stable and loving character

Black silver blotched queen

The average Maine Coon litter will have four kittens, but seven or eight is certainly no exception. You must realize that if you breed a litter, each and every kitten will deserve a loving new home and that raising and socializing a large litter will take a great deal of time. The breeder of your queen is the obvious person to support you in all aspects of breeding. The owner of the stud tom will also be able to help, as will the breed association. At the end of the day, though, you as breeder will be responsible for the quality and health of the kittens – and liable for any future problems. So consider all the pros and cons carefully before you decide to breed, and make sure that you are fully aware of what's ahead.

The average litter will have four kittens, but larger or smaller litters are also quite common

Genetic diversity

Genetic diversity is important if any species or subspecies of animal is to remain healthy. In scientific terms the Maine Coon as a breed is a subspecies of the domestic cat. Breeders of every breed of cat know that inbreeding, i.e. cross breeding of related animals, reduces the genetic diversity of the breed. This can reduce the genetic resistance, while the increased homozygosity – which means

that animals increasingly have the same genes – can (unintentionally) increase the occurrence of hereditary abnormalities in family lines. Maine Coon breeders are well aware that they are working with a breed that, in terms of registration, is very young indeed. Since the fifties, some hundred different farm cats from the Maine region have been registered in the pedigree registers as Maine Coons. These form the basis, the foundation of the breed and are therefore called the 'foundation cats'. Yet now, fifty years on, it proves that only five of them worldwide make up the majority (between 65 and 75%) of the family background. This is in part due to the fact that some of the offspring of those five cats (also known as the 'clones') inherited so well that breeders chose to continue breeding with

Brown tabby queen

them. The offspring of those clones, with their uniform type, their large size and prominently shaped head, were particular favorites with the judges, so that they are behind almost all lines. Nowadays, breeders aiming to safeguard genetic diversity, i.e. genetic health, are careful to ensure that the percentages of inbreeding, of 'top five cats,' and of clones, are kept as low as possible, to keep the breed a healthy one in future.

The Top Five Cats

The top five of the foundation cats featuring the most often in Main Coon pedigrees, in order, are:

1. *Andy Katt of Heidi Ho*
2. *Bridget Katt of Heidi Ho*
3. *Dauphin de France of Tati-Tan*
4. *Tatiana of Tati-Tan*
5. *Smokie Joe of Whittemore*

Breeding "New Blood"

As we have already explained, as a breed the present Maine Coon was created from non-breed cats that lived on the east coast of the United States. For the purpose of (re)creating the breed, these cats were registered. In later years too, cats that complied with certain criteria could be registered in the pedigree to maximize the genetic diversity. However, in 1980s most of the large pedigree organizations in the United States closed the pedigree for the Maine Coon. So from then on, no non-pedigree ('foundation') cats were allowed into the breed. This limited the possibility for breeders to register non-pedigree Maine Coons from Maine and the surrounding area, and meant that inbreeding continued with a stock founded on relatively few animals. Over the last decade however, a great deal has been done to keep the breed genetically healthy. Maine Coon breeders are remarkably active in this respect compared with other breeds. Databases have been set up on the Internet enabling anybody to trace the exact line of descent of his or her cats. Linked to the databases are calculation programs to work out how inbred a particular cat is, and whether a proposed parent couple would increase or reduce the percentage of inbreeding. The percentage of clones of the top-five cats present in a particu-

Eleven-week old kitten

lar cat's pedigree can also be calculated. In addition several people from the United States and Germany have returned to Maine. From farms and families there they selected suitable, longhaired, new foundation kittens and cats. These cats have been registered with the ACA, one of the smaller pedigree organizations, because the ACA still allows the registration of non-pedigree cats from the Maine region. Offspring from these cats, combined with the existing population, will bring new blood into the Maine Coon breed so that it will remain a healthy breed in future. In several countries in Europe various new-foundation lines are now available. So if you decide to breed, do make a point of checking on the Internet to find out how inbred your queen is. At the same time look to see if the tom you have chosen has produced kittens that are preferably less related, in terms of inbreeding percentage, than both parent animals.

Page 99
Black silver tabby
queen with "van"
marking

9 COLORS

Color variations

The first Maine Coon breeders used to say: 'You have to build your house before you can paint it'. By that they meant that the breed type was the most important aspect of the Maine Coon and that the coloring was of secondary importance. Contrary to what is common practice for other breeds, the Maine Coon breed standards specify little or nothing about color. There are some people who prefer to breed particular color variations. Those tints will either be personal favorites or ones they personally believe best suit the breed. So the selection of colors and patterns really is incidental, although some Maine Coon breeders do their best to achieve an attractive pattern and a warm color. The Maine Coon is bred in a wide range of colors and patterns but not in all colors and patterns seen in other cats. Generally speaking, color and pattern genes of so-called Oriental origin, such as the chocolate, cinnamon, ticked tabby and the partial albinism factors seen in Burmese and Siamese coloring, are considered undesirable. In the opinion of the breed experts, who classify the

The color of
Maine Coons
is of secondary
importance; all
degrees of white
are allowed

*Red is one
of the two base
colors in cats*

Maine Coon as a natural farm cat, these colors are not Maine Coon colors.

The base colors

The various coat colors in cats are formed by tiny pigment granules in the hair. The granules vary in shape and size, and they can be differently grouped in the shaft of the hair shaft and in different places in the hair.

*The spotted
marking is clearly
visible in this
black smoke and
white kitten*

These pigment granules are called melanins. All "base colors" seen in cats (with the exception of white) are made up from two types of pigment: eumelanin (black) and phaeomelanin (red/orange). In the Maine Coon we also see a dilute factor (d). If this is doubly present (dd), it causes the pigment granules to coagulate in the hair shaft. The result is a space between the pigment granules and the color fades. Black fades to an optical blue (gray), red becomes cream and tortie becomes bluecream.

Ghost Marking in Solid-Colored Cats

Most solid-colored kittens have a light tabby marking in their coat that is known as 'ghost marking'. This usually fades as the kitten grows up and will have disappeared altogether within a year. Very occasionally the vague, tabby marking will remain visible in an adult cat, particularly on the tail and sometimes the legs. Red and cream cats form an exception. It is impossible to say if these colors are tabby or not, as the tabby pattern will always

Ten-month old black smoke and white tom

remain visible, regardless of whether or not the cat is an agouti.

Smoke

The smoke group consists of solid color cats (i.e. solid red, black, blue, crème, tortie or bluecream) with a silvery white undercoat. This silvery white undercoat is caused by the dominantly inherited I gene. In most cats with this inhibitor gene, half the hair will be decolorized from the root up, but some are only partially decolorized or decolorized in patches (the so-called "low-grade smokes").

Tabbies

Three different tabby patterns are seen in Maine Coons: "blotched," "mackerel" and "spotted." The gene controlling the spotted tabby pattern is inherited independ-

The blotched pattern is the most common tabby pattern seen in the Maine Coon

ently of the mackerel or blotched tabby patterns, and causes the pattern to break into spots. The tabby pattern is created by a combination of genes. Firstly, the cat must carry an agouti gene A to reveal the genetically present tabby pattern. Other genes then determine which patterns are revealed. Silver tabbies also carry the inhibitor

gene I, which gives the tabby pattern a silvery white undercoat.

Shell-and-shaded

The shell-and-shaded group was originally silver tabbies where, for generations, selective breeding crossed cats with the vaguest of tabby patterns—and indeed still does. The resulting cats have tabby patterns that have become so vague they are little more than a veil or "shade" on top of the silverwhite undercoat. The optically lighter versions are called "shell," the heavier—and therefore apparently darker—versions are called "shaded." Because this is polygenetically determined, it is perfectly normal for there to be both shell and shaded kittens in one and the same litter. A shell or shaded cat that doesn't carry the silver factor I, is called "golden shell" or "golden shaded."

Genuine shaded or shell cats are still extremely rare in Maine Coons

Bicolor, Tricolor, Harlequin and Van

The bicolor, tricolor, harlequin and van groups, include all the cats with white markings. In these colors, a little or a lot of the coat is decolorized (i.e., white). The amount of white can vary considerably: from a cat with a tiny little white flash on its tummy to a cat that is almost entirely white, bar a bit of color on its tail and on the top of its head. Bicolors and tricolors are cats where one–third to half of the cat is white. Cats with a great deal of white are called "harlequins" or "vans." The latter have just a little color on the top of their heads and/or a few patches on their back and/or a colored tail. Cats with quite a lot of white in their coat can also have odd eyes (two different colors) or blue eyes. The amount of white in the coat is completely random, and no two are the same as far as the percentage or distribution of white. The amount of white can be increased though, by continually mating cats with a lot of white, and then only breeding with pure white offspring. The partial decolorization of the coat is caused by the S gene.

White

A solid white coat is caused by the dominant W gene. This gene inhibits the production of color pigment in the hair shaft, so that the cat appears to be white. In a way, the cat is "wearing a white shroud" over its natural color/pat-

A white cat can produce both white and colored kittens

Page 107
This kitten will
eventually be
'ordinary' black
when it's mature

tern combination. A white cat can produce both white and colored kittens. A copper-eyed cat may have eyes of any shade from green to yellow to orange. Young, solid white kittens often have a colored patch between the ears that fades with age. This colored patch is the true color the cat of under the white at that spot.

Colors

• **White**
Copper-eyed white, odd-eyed white, blue-eyed white

• **Solid**
Black, blue, red, cream, black tortie, bluecream

• **Smoke**
Black smoke, blue smoke, red smoke, cream smoke, black tortie smoke, bluecream smoke

• **Tabbies**
Black tabby, blue tabby, red tabby, cream tabby, black tortie tabby, bluecream tabby

• **Silver Tabbies**
Black silver tabby, blue silver tabby, red silver tabby, cream silver tabby, black tortie silver tabby, bluecream silver tabby

• **Shell and shaded**
Black shell/shaded silver, blue shell/shaded silver, red shell/shaded silver, cream shell/shaded silver, black tortie shell/shaded silver, bluecream shell/shaded silver, black shell/shaded golden, blue shell/shaded golden, black tortie shell/shaded golden, bluecream shell/shaded golden, red shell/shaded golden and cream shell/shaded golden

• **Bicolor, tricolor, harlequin, and van**
All the above colors (except solid white) have some white in the coat

10 GENETICS

Knowledge of
genetics will enable
you to predict the
possible colors of
the kittens

A brief look at genetics

For anyone breeding cats, it is useful to have some basic knowledge of genetics. This will enable them to examine the pedigrees of the parent animals and calculate what colors the kittens will be, or what patterns they will have. It also gives the breeder some insight into the function of other genetic factors and the way in which they are passed on from generation to generation. Cats carry all their genetic information on their chromosomes that come in pairs. A cat has 38 chromosomes (i.e., 19 pairs). One of

those pairs of chromosomes determines the sex of the kitten. A tom has one X and one Y chromosome and a queen has two X chromosomes. In his testes, the tom produces spermatozoa, each of which contains half of his chromosomes. In her ovaries, the queen produces ova (egg cells), each of which also contains half of her chromosomes. After mating, the released ova fuse with the sperm, so that the resulting kittens get half their genetic qualities from their mother and the other half from their father.

Genes

The chromosomes carry the genes. These are tiny isolated pieces of hereditary information that contain all the codes to determine what the animal will look like, both on the inside and the outside. This relates to both appearance, such as the shape of the head, the color and length of the, and things like hereditary resistance against illness and other characteristics. Not all characteristics are hereditary and most can be modified to a certain degree. Although a cat that is naturally withdrawn will become decidedly timid if it is not cared for properly, the same cat, with good, loving care will still never lose that "slight shyness" it was born with. The most knowledge there is about the genetics of cats relates to the inheritance of the colors and patterns of the coat.

Phenotype and Genotype

Phenotype: the exterior (i.e. the cat's appearance)
Genotype: the cat's complete package of genes, both the factors it reveals and the factors it carries unseen but can pass on to its offspring.

Dominant and recessive

For each trait, a kitten gets one gene from its mother and one from its father, so it has two genes for every trait. Every trait determined by a specific gene has a counterpart. One trait is "dominant" and is, therefore, revealed in the animal's appearance, while the other trait is "recessive" and is not revealed. A trait the animal does not reveal can, nevertheless, be passed on to its offspring. An example of this is the gene "d" that controls a dilute coat color. This gene is recessive, which means that it can only be expressed in the cat's appearance if there is no dominant counterpart to repress it. So a recessive trait can only be expressed if the cat has inherited that gene from both parents. The dominant counterpart of "d" is "D"; which

Two recessive traits in one animal: long hair and a dilute coat color

represents a solid, non-dilute color. A cat carrying the genotype DD will have a non-dilute colored coat, as will a cat carrying the genotype Dd. The latter will still carry the dilute factor though, and will, therefore, be able to pass it on to his or her offspring. Only cats with the genotype dd will have a dilute colored coat. Cats that are homozygous for a particular trait have two identical genes (e.g. DD or dd), and cats that are heterozygous for a particular trait have two different genes (e.g. Dd).

This black blotched tom could also produce blue, non-tabby kittens

Polygenetic

Some hereditary factors are determined by several tiny pieces of genetic information, as opposed to the single-gene (monogenetic) factors described above. Traits that are determined by more than one piece of genetic information are called polygenetic traits. An example of a polygenetic trait is the shade of a black cat. This can vary from a pitch black to a rusty or even reddish black. The shade is controlled by various polygenes that influence the main trait "black."

Genetic Symbols

Since the 1950s, letters have been used to denote the genetic traits determined by a specific gene. The "nomenclature" for the cat was laid down by an international commission, presided over by the late feline geneticist, Roy Robinson. Over the years, as additional knowledge and insight was acquired, the nomenclature was expanded and amended. A dominant, monogenetic trait is always denoted by a capital letter, the recessive counterpart with a lower-case letter. The following list gives factors relevant to the Maine Coon:

The tabby pattern of this red shaded kitten has practically disappeared as a result of polygenes

* A = Agouti / a = non-agouti:
This gene determines whether or not the cat's coat will actually reveal a particular tabby pattern.
A makes this possible, a will mean that the cat will not reveal a tabby pattern in its coat and will, therefore, be a "solid" color.

* D = Dense / d = non-dense:
D is the factor that in the recessive form and the homozygous form (dd) causes the pigment granules to coagulate, creating a dilute color. Black becomes blue, red becomes cream, and tortie (red and black) becomes bluecream.

* I = Inhibited / i = non-inhibited:
I is the pigment inhibitor that causes the hair roots to decolorize. The decolorized sections of the hair contain no pigment granules. A cat with a tabby pattern will become a silver tabby and a solid colored cat with a silver-white undercoat is called a "smoke."

* L = shorthair / l = longhair:
All Maine Coons are longhaired, so they all have the genotype ll.

* Mc = mackerel tabby pattern / mc = blotched/classic tabby pattern:
The dominant form of the tabby pattern is mackerel, a striped pattern. The recessive counterpart creates a marbled pattern with large, round blotches on the cat's sides.

Page 114
Without the two d genes, this bluecream and white cat would have been black tortie and white.

White spots are caused by the Sp gene

* S = Piebald Spotting / s = non-piebald spotting:
If the cat carries the S gene, parts of its coat will have no pigment and, accordingly, be white.

* Sp = spotted / sp = non-spotted:
This gene will break the tabby pattern into spots

* Pd = polydactyl / pd = non-polydactyl:
Pd is the trait that gives the cat extra toes.

* W = White / w = non-white:
The W gene determines a solid white cat, whereby the production of pigment in the hair is completely inhibited.

* XO = orange / Xo = non-orange:
The two base colors red and black are on the cat's sexual chromosomes. O means that orange pigment (phaeomelanin) will be produced, and o means that black pigment (eumelanin) will be produced. There is no dominance between the two. A queen (XX) can manifest both traits,

The W gene determines a solid white cat

and be XOXo. So she would be tortoise colored. Toms (XY) only have one X-chromosome, so they are always either red or black.

Red queen

Long codes

A genetic code for a particular cat consists of an alphabetical list indicating exactly which factors the cat has manifested and which it is carrying. There is usually one dominant type and one recessive counterpart, sometimes there are two dominant types that correlate intermediately, and sometimes there are two or three recessive counterparts that may or may not be in a particular order. Some breeders specify the genetic codes of their stud animals on their homepage on the Internet. With a little puzzling, even a beginner can start to comprehend what the codes mean. An example: a black-blotched and white tom born of a black with white and blue-blotched parent would have the following genetic code, in respect of his color, pattern, and markings:

Aa-Dd-ii-mcmc-Ss-ww-XoY

GLOSSARY

A

ACA: American Cat Association, one of the smaller pedigree organizations for cats in the United States, that still allows the registration of new "farm cats" from Maine.

Agouti gene: if the A gene is present, any tabby pattern the cat has will be revealed in its coat.

B

Bacterium: a sometimes pathogenic single-cell organism that often lives in other organisms. There are useful and harmful bacteria.

Bicolor: literally "two colors." The term is used for cats that have between 33% and 50% white in their coat and one other main color, either with or without a tabby pattern.

All Maine Coons with white in their coat are parti-colors

A brown tabby

Blue: dilute version of the main color black that occurs if the recessive gene for dilute is doubly present (dd). The cat actually looks gray, but the term "blue" was chosen in the cat world back in the nineteenth century and is still used today.

Bluecream: dilute version of the coat color tortie. Synonym: bluetortie.

Bluetortie: synonym for bluecream.

Blotched: a marbled version of the tabby.

Breeder: anyone who breeds a litter with a purebred cat.

Breed standard: detailed description, established by international feline associations, specifying exactly what a particular breed of cat should look like.

C

Carnivore: meat eater, an animal whose natural diet consists primarily of animals of prey.

Castration: term denoting the sterilization of either the queen or the tom, by removing the reproductive organs.

Cattery name: official "surname" given to every kitten bred by a particular breeder. The breeder registers the name of his or her choice with a feline association and the name can then be added either in front of (prefix) or after (suffix) the kitten's own name.

CFA: Cat Fanciers Association. The largest feline federation in America.

Classic: American name for the blotched tabby.

Clones: the much-used offspring of the five first ancestors of the breed and ancestors of many Maine Coons.

Cream: dilute version of the main color red that occurs if the recessive gene for dilute is doubly present (dd). The cat actually looks beige, but the cat world chose the term cream a long time ago.

D

Dilute: hereditary recessive trait that is only expressed if the cat carries the gene d twice. The pigment granules in the hair shaft coagulate, optically bleaching the base color.

Dominant gene: a hereditary trait that is expressed phenotypically, even if it is only singularly present in the cat's genetic make-up.

E

Eumelanin: black pigment granules in the hair shaft.

F

Feeding at random: a term used to describe a situation where the cat has constant access to food and can, therefore, eat as and when it wants to.

Feline Acne: local skin condition where overactive sebaceous glands cause blackheads and sometimes bacterial inflammation

Young cream and white tom

Five-year old black silver tortie blotched queen

FIFé: Federation International Feline. The largest feline federation in Europe.
Foundation cat: a registered Maine Coon from the region of origin.
Foundation line: the term for the family line bred from foundation cats.

G
Gene: the carrier of hereditary information.
Genotype: the complete package of genes of a particular cat, so all the factors it expresses, but also the ones it carries unseen but could still pass on to its offspring.
Golden: collective term for all non-silver cats with shading polygenes, born of shell or shaded-silver parents.

H
Harlequin: coat pattern with color on the top of the head, the tail, and no more than three patches on the rest of the body, the rest of the coat being white.
Heat: when a queen is in her fertile period, which happens several times a year and usually lasts from a few days to two weeks, she is said to be "in heat."
Heterozygous: this term is used if the cat has two different

genes for a particular trait. The cat's phenotype is not the same as its genotype.

Homozygous: this term is used if both genes for a particular trait are identical. The trait will always be expressed in the cat's appearance.

I

Inbreeding: Crossing two very closely related animals, such as brother x sister, mother x son, father x daughter or half-brother x half-sister.

Inhibitor-factor: dominantly inherited gene that inhibits the pigmentation of part of the coat from the base (root), resulting in a silver-white undercoat.

J

Jowls: overdeveloped cheeks seen in toms, caused by hormones, that disappear after castration.

L

Line breeding: a breeders' euphemism for inbreeding, often used for mating between slightly less related animals such as grandfather x granddaughter or cousin x cousin.

M

Mackerel: name given to the striped tabby pattern.

N

Non-agouti: the lack of possibility to express the tabby pattern present, so that the coat appears to have no pattern at all (solid).

Neuter: to remove the testicles or ovaries of an animal.

O

Odd-eyed: two different colored eyes, one blue and one copper, seen in solid white cats and sometimes cats with a lot of white in their coats, such as harlequins and vans.

Outcross: crossing two animals of the same breed that are practically unrelated.

P

Parti-colors: a name used to refer to the group of cats that have a certain amount of white in their coats, besides a solid main color. The group includes bicolors, tricolors, harlequins, and vans.

Pedigree: official certificate, issued by an authorized feline association or federation that specifies the line of ancestors over four, or sometimes five generations. Belongs to the individual cat.

Phaeomelanin: red pigment granules in the hair shaft.

Phenotype: the exterior, the cat's appearance.

Points: recessive hereditary partial albinism factor that means that a cat only displays any color at the very extremities (head, ears and tail). Of Oriental origin and therefore disallowed in the Maine Coon.

Polygenetic: some hereditary factors are determined by several tiny individual pieces of genetic information, as opposed to one gene (monogenetic).

R

Recessive gene: a hereditary trait that will only be phenotypically expressed if the cat has inherited the factor from both parents.

Ruff: longer hair round the neck.

S

Shaded: tabby pattern where, following generations of selective breeding, the tabby pattern has faded to a "shade."

Shaggy: describes the character of the Maine Coon's coat.

Shell: the polygenetically lighter form of shaded.

Smoke: solid (non-agouti) cat with a silver white undercoat caused by the I gene.

Spay: to surgically remove an animal's ovaries and adjacent parts of the uterus

Spotted: the spotted tabby pattern.

Sterilization: rendering a tom or queen infertile while preserving the reproductive organs. In practice neither toms nor queens are ever sterilized, although the term is often used in layman's speech when referring to spaying.

Stud tail: sticky, brown substance, at the top of the tail of an unneutered tom or queen, caused by overactive sebaceous glands, as a result of increased hormone levels.

T

Tabby: coat pattern expressed by the presence of the agouti gene. Occurs in Maine Coons in blotched, striped and spotted varieties.

TICA: The International Cat Association, a large, fairly new feline federation in America where many Maine Coons are registered and showed.

Ticked Tabby: Oriental variety of the tabby pattern where only the agouti hairs are visible and no clear pattern can be seen. Because of its Oriental origin, it is classified as a fault in the Maine Coon.

Tortie: (also called tortoise or tortoiseshell) the name given to a mottled pattern of euumelanin and phaeomelanin, i.e. red and black pigments in the coat. Seen in queens only.

Tortietabby: A combination of tortie and tabby.

Tortoiseshell: see tortie.

U

Undershot mouth: the bottom jaw is longer than the top jaw so that the teeth do not close properly

V

Van: a white cat with one or two patches of color on its head and a colored tail.

Virus: the smallest infectious pathogen, made up of a string of DNA, that tries to multiply in its host, damaging his or her health in the process.

A silver tabby has at least one inhibitor gene that decolorizes the undercoat

USEFUL ADDRESSES

Breed Association

Useful Internet Addresses

• Database of genetic abnormalities: www.fomcc.org
An on-line file of Maine Coons with test results for HCM, PKD, HD and PL

• The History of the Maine Coon: bowen1.home.mind-spring.com/mchs/home.htm
Maine Coon Heritage Site about origins, kinship and genetic variations

• Hip Dysplasia: www.offa.org/hdcat.html
Information on HD tests for cats by OFA, Orthopedic Foundation For Animals.

• HCM: members.aol.com/jchinitz/hcm/
Info pages about HCM in cats

• PKD: www.felinepkd.com
Info pages about PKD in cats

• PL/HD: fhda.com/
Info pages about HD and PL in cats

• The largest American Breed Association: www.mcbfa.org.

Red Maine
Coon queen

Thanks and Photo Credits

All the photos were made by Furry Tails.nl/ Esther Verhoef, except: Marian Draat: pages 12, 13, 25, 57, 90, 118, 128; Astrid s and Leo Straver: pages 14, 32 above, 38, 78, 122, 125; Marga Harms: pages 29, 36, 40, 56, 75, 105; Francien Verspui: pages 33.
All the black and white photos were taken from The Book of the Cat (1903) by Frances Simpson.

The author and publisher wish to thank Astrid Straver, for reading sections of the manuscript and offering many valuable suggestions and comments on the subject of breeding Maine Coons. We also wish to thank all the other breeders and owners who provided the author with information on keeping and caring for Maine Coons. Last but not least, we wish to thank all breeders and owners who were kind enough to photograph their cats, or allow us to do so. The owners of the cats illustrated, at the time they were photographed, included Marga Harms, Astrid and Leo Straver, Monique van Stuijvenberg, Thea Stigter, José Kerkhofs, and Carin and Sebastian Poos.

White tom